Where is God in my Suffering?

DANIEL J. SIMUNDSON

Where is God in my Suffering?

Biblical Responses to Seven Searching Questions

AUGSBURG Publishing House • Minneapolis

WHERE IS GOD IN MY SUFFERING?

Preface

At times of suffering the mind is flooded with questions: Why is this happening to me? Have I ever done anything so bad that I should be punished this way? Has God abandoned me? Doesn't God love me anymore? Can't God do something about my troubles? Where are all my so-called friends now that I need them? What is there to hope for—more of the present pain and grief and loneliness, and finally death? Where is God in all of this?

We cannot turn off our minds. The questions keep coming. How can we find answers? Or if not answers, how can we find peace?

In this book we shall look at several of the questions most often raised by people who are suffering.

We shall examine them in the light of specific biblical texts. And we shall attempt to see how the gospel story of the death of Jesus on the cross sheds light on our experience of suffering.

This book could be used in various ways. It could be helpful to a pastor planning a series of sermons on suffering, either during Lent or some other time of the year. Lay people and pastors might find some insights that will help them in their search for meaning in suffering, whether it be in their own lives or in the lives of others to whom they wish to speak a word of comfort. An adult class could use this book to study the perennial human problem of how to understand and endure suffering.

God invites us to raise our questions, not to back off from the search for meaning in our suffering. But even as we open our mouths to form the questions, we know in our hearts that many of them will remain unanswered. There are limits to human understanding. There are mysteries which cannot be rationalized into logical clarity. When we are acutely aware of our limitations before the mysteries of God, we ask God's presence to give us peace and the ability to cope with suffering that will neither be explained nor go away.

CHAPTER 1

Do I
Deserve This?

Exodus 34:6-7; John 9:1-7

"Do I deserve this?" is one of the most common
reactions to suffering. The world should make sense.
God is good, and God is in charge. Good things are
supposed to come to good people and bad things to
bad people. The presence of suffering then raises
questions of blame and gives us the feeling of being
punished. Am I really that bad? Have I been such
a great sinner? Have I been fooling myself into
thinking I was better than I really am? Maybe I
need to probe more deeply into my inner self to
see if there is sin which needs to be confessed and
forgiven. If I am not bad enough to deserve this,
does that mean that God is unfair? None of us is
happy with either thought—either that we are bad
enough to deserve this or that God is unfair.

Many religious people turn inward at times of trouble. They do not want to blame God for their troubles, and so, in a search for answers, they accuse themselves. Often the more religious we are, the more likely we are to blame ourselves for our suffering.

The Bible often blames humans for their suffering

People who know the Bible best sometimes have the most trouble with the question, "Do I deserve this?" because many biblical passages interpret the suffering of human beings as a consequence of their sin. Genesis 3, the story of the fall, says that suffering, pain, hard work, and death come into the world as a result of the disobedience of the man and the woman—with a little help from the snake. God had made a good world. It should have remained a lovely and pleasant place, a paradise where no one would have to suffer. But Adam and Eve did not trust God's command to stay away from the forbidden tree, and so the world became as it is now instead of the way it could have been.

The historians who recorded the story of Israel and Judah in the books of Kings understood that those nations went down to defeat before other countries because they had turned away from God, followed after other gods, and abused the weak and poor and helpless in their own society. There was a reason for the disaster of the exile. The reason was the sin of the people which had to be punished.

The great Old Testament prophets also made connections between the sins that people committed and the trouble which would soon come upon them. Similar ideas can be found in Proverbs and some of the psalms: the world makes sense, and sin leads to unpleasant consequences. The three friends who came to counsel Job also were convinced of the power and fairness of God, and they could not believe that God would let an innocent person suffer. Therefore, they assumed that Job must have been a sinner after all. As good as he seemed, there must have been something in Job's life that he needed to confess to clear the air so that God could forgive him and bring back the good life.

When people suffer, they remember these texts. They wonder if God might be punishing them as God once punished those people in biblical times.

Maybe I really deserve what is happening to me

Often we are too quick to allow ourselves and others to escape personal responsibility. Adam said, "The woman that you gave to be with me made me do it." And Eve said, "The serpent tricked me." They both tried to pass the buck.

Today, too, people find ways of saying, "It's not my fault." "Someone else got me into this." "It's the fault of my parents who didn't give me enough love when I was growing up." Or, "My parents gave me too much love and wouldn't let me take a few lumps of my own. They kept me too dependent on them." We might blame our neighbors or all those in authority—politicians, church bureaucrats, big business or big labor, or generals in plushy offices who coldly calculate how to fight the next world war. Surely there are enough others out there to blame for our troubles.

Maybe we should at least consider the possibility that there is something to this old biblical belief that sinners bring suffering on themselves. We do things that contribute to our own problems. We are unable to love as we ought, and therefore we are not loved as we wish. Our habits of eating and drinking and smoking and avoiding exercise and living stressful lives make us susceptible to physical ills of one kind or another. There may be connections between our emotional and spiritual and physical lives that we are only beginning to understand. In ways still unknown to us, we may even be responsible for some of our own diseases. Though we may not identify our suffering as the result of sin nor speak of God taking an active role in bringing the suffering as punishment, it still remains true that certain behavior will lead to certain consequences. We cannot do whatever we please in our lives—in relationship to others or with regard to our own bodies—without someday having to pay the price.

So we ought not be too quick to dismiss the question—"Do I deserve this?"—as if it were an antiquated way of thinking in our modern world, or as if any suggestion of sin or guilt or personal responsibility is unhealthy for human beings. At times of suffering, it may be appropriate to ask what we have done to contribute to the situation. There is still a need for personal responsibility, for confession, for forgiveness. We cannot blame others for everything that has gone wrong in our lives. Some of it might be our own fault.

God expects us to be responsible and doesn't allow us to beg off and claim we couldn't help ourselves. God made a world that makes sense. We can study the world and see some of the connections. We can learn some of the things that cause suffering so that we can avoid them and help others avoid them. We can find new cures for illnesses. We can change our life-styles so that we can live happier and healthier lives. When suffering does come, we can learn from experience and perhaps prevent a recurrence.

Not all suffering is a result of sin

Having said all this, it still remains true that we cannot understand all suffering as a result of sin. Certainly we cannot look at the suffering of a specific human being and point out some sin that has either caused the trouble or has moved God to bring some punishment. We cannot necessarily locate the reason for every cancer, heart attack, or tragic accident. Many religious people suffer even more than is necessary, because they are troubled by guilt which is unwarranted, because they feel condemned for getting into trouble, because they begin to think of God as one who sends punishment rather than as the one who brings comfort. People have read the biblical texts that explain certain examples of suffering as payment for sin, and then they apply those same conclusions to the misfortunes in their own lives.

But it is not necessarily true that all suffering is a result of sin. It is one thing to say that disobedience to God will cause suffering. It is implying much more to say that *all* suffering is the result of sin. You cannot always work backwards from the suffering and suppose a specific cause. Nothing works out that simply in this complex life. Maybe the sin that brought you trouble is the sin of someone else—a family member who mistreated you, a boss who is mean and vindictive, a drunken driver who caused the accident, the failure of our leaders to prevent a war. Maybe there is such a thing as innocent suffering—people who just happen to be in the wrong place at the wrong time. Job is certainly an example of one who did not deserve all that was happening to him, though his counselors tried to make him look bad in order to protect their theory that people should suffer in this life only as they deserve.

The book of Job is only one of the places where the Bible raises objections to those who want to explain every case of suffering as a result of sin. There are other alternatives to a cruel and indiscriminate application of a theory of retribution. Maybe our suffering has some greater purpose, either for ourselves (discipline, educational value, protecting me from future dangers) or for others. Maybe it is the work of hostile, demonic forces. Maybe it is simply a mystery, one that will never be solved, and the best thing for us to do is to look for peace and faith in God even in the midst of a world that does not provide easy answers to our most important questions.

Maybe 1, 2, or 3,

Jesus brings us a word of freedom

Sometimes we run from responsibility, blaming others for our troubles, refusing to take action to make the world more pleasant for ourselves and those around us. At such times the word of cause and effect between what we do and what happens to us needs to be heard. At other times, we are only too aware of our guilt and our responsibility for our troubles. Then we need someone to tell us that our pain is not our own fault and God is not our enemy, searching to find new and ever more creative ways of punishing us.

In either case, Jesus brings us a word of relief. If we have in fact brought our own sin upon us, Jesus comes with forgiveness. It is painful to look at ourselves with clear eyes and see all those times when we have hurt others and hurt ourselves. But since God has forgiven us in Jesus Christ, we can dare to face our darkest selves, open up to God honestly, and make our confession, knowing that God loves sinners and will forgive.

For those who are deeply troubled by the doctrine of retribution, who fear a God who seems more like a condemning judge than a loving parent, the sacrifice of Jesus on the cross becomes a powerful symbol of how we can be freed from the consequences of our sins. Jesus has suffered for us. He has taken our place. He has accepted our punishment. He died for us that we might be forgiven and not have to suffer the fate that our sins deserve. Since we all are sinners, we all could be suffering—if not in this life, then after this life. But we are assured by the death of Jesus on the cross that God will not punish us forever. God will forgive and accept us and bring us comfort.

Jesus also has a word for those who need to be freed from excessive imagined guilt. Jesus can help us rise above self-condemnation so that we can make proper distinctions about when to feel guilty and when not to blame ourselves. Not all suffering has the same cause. Certainly each individual example of suffering cannot be traced to a specific sin. Jesus can give us the wisdom to sort that out: to accept blame where appropriate and seek forgiveness, not to assume guilt where it does not seem correct. Every case of suffering is different. We must not try to force a neat answer in every situation, as Job's counselors did with poor Job.

One of the best places to find a word of Jesus on this subject is in John 9. Jesus and his disciples passed by a blind man. The disciples asked Jesus, "Who sinned, this man or his parents, that he was born blind?" (John 9:2). That is a logical question if you assume that there is always some human being at fault in every example of suffering. Like many people in our own day, Jesus' disciples had read their Bible (our Old Testament) and they knew some of those same texts that we have talked about earlier, and they assumed a human responsibility for suffering. Jesus responded by saying that the blindness was not the result of sins on the part of either the blind man or his parents, but "that the works of God might be made manifest in him" (John 9:3). The question of blame is irrelevant. The important point is that God will make himself known by responding to the need of this blind man.

And so it is with our suffering. Maybe we have done something to deserve it. If so, it is good to be aware of that, to admit it, and be forgiven. But maybe we are innocent. We cannot see why it should be happening to us and not to someone else who appears to be a worse sinner than we are. It may be irrelevant to raise the question of blame. The suffering is there, wherever it came from, and God is there to meet our needs for comfort. That is what is important.

"Do I deserve this?" If the answer is yes, Jesus brings forgiveness. If the answer is no, Jesus brings us a word of relief from the compulsion to see all suffering as punishment—a word that frees us from the guilt of blaming ourselves for our troubles.

17

CHAPTER 2

My God, Why Have You Forsaken Me?

Psalm 22

Bad things happen to Christians too. We are not immune from the misfortunes of life. Sickness, pain, disappointment, economic losses, emotional disturbances, and death are no respecter of persons. We are all vulnerable. Suffering is not confined to those "who deserve it."

And, like other human beings, we Christians don't like it when bad things happen to us. Like others who are hurt in a deep way, we respond with anger, fear, despair, and rejection. In some ways, Christians may react even more negatively to adversity, because we may have thought that our pious life-styles and trust in God's providence would protect us from the unpleasantness of life and bring us safely to the glorious life that is to come. If we have trusted that faith in God is a kind of insurance policy to keep away trouble, then it is not surprising to be overcome with a sense of outrage, as if God has lied or at best forgotten about us.

What are we to do when we are consumed with negative feelings and thoughts? Many have found it difficult to express them. You attempt to tell another believer that you are beginning to doubt the existence of God, or, if God does exist, he must not care much about people to let them suffer like this. But you can barely get the words out of your mouth before you are hushed up and advised not to think like that anymore. You try to explain how empty you are inside since your spouse died, but your friend keeps interrupting you, trying to cheer you up, telling you it is not good for you to indulge in such self-pity. Though you can feel only sadness, your friend keeps reminding you how good it is to be a believer so that you are not like other persons who have no hope. But, inside, you feel like those other persons who have no hope.

Good religious people also suffer. And when they do, they have negative thoughts and feelings. And they do not have much help in dealing with them, because there seems to be an overwhelming desire on the part of almost everyone to keep them from expressing, or even admitting, what is going on inside of themselves at times of suffering. They are not allowed to say boldly and publicly, "My God, why have you forsaken me?"

20

There is some biblical material that could be very helpful to us in times of suffering. It is the biblical *lament*, a prayer offered up to God in times of deep trouble. As we have stifled the efforts of an individual sufferer to speak about negative thoughts, so also we have squelched the use of laments. They seem unnatural and unduly pessimistic to most of us. We leave them out of our hymnbooks and don't use them in worship. If we happen to stumble across them as we read through our Bibles, we wonder what such negative, uninspiring stuff is doing in the Scriptures.

Let us think about laments, why they have been neglected and how they could be helpful to a sufferer. We will use excerpts from Psalm 22 for most of our examples of a lament.

Why the lament has been stifled

There is no question that we Christians are uncomfortable with laments, whether they are the spontaneous complaints of an acquaintance or the more formal lament psalms found in the Bible. Why should this be? Here are a few possibilities:

We don't like them because they are bad psychology. When we are confronted by a morbid, complaining, self-pitying outburst from someone, we tend to respond by trying to change that person's outlook, trying to cheer him up, seeking to bring her to a more positive outlook. "Don't talk like

21

that. Don't think like that. Things can't be that bad. Don't feel so sorry for yourself." Those are our typical reactions to such statements as: "I am a worm and no man; scorned by men, and despised by the people" (Ps. 22:6). "I am poured out like water, and all my bones are out of joint; my heart is like wax, it is melted within my breast; my strength is dried up like a potsherd" (Ps. 22:14-15a).

Our motive is to help the one who laments. The words sound so terrible, the feelings expressed are so unpleasant, that we want to eliminate them, to divert the sufferer away from such thinking. And so we don't want to hear the lament. We think it cannot do anyone any good to talk like this. Certainly, we think, we do not want to provide people words, from the Bible or elsewhere, that will encourage them to continue in their negative frame of mind.

We don't like them because they are bad theology. To a sufferer, God often seems distant, uncaring, inaccessible. "My God, my God, why hast thou forsaken me? Why art thou so far from helping me, from the words of my groaning? O my God, I cry by day, but thou dost not answer; and by night, but find no rest" (Ps. 22:1-2). Where are we to look for God? Has God left us forever? The old prayers seem so empty—like talking to ourselves or going through the motions without any meaning. How can a sufferer recover the sense of intimacy

22

with God that used to be there? Right now, when the presence of God is most urgently needed, it is farther away than it has ever been.

The laments often describe God as absent, cruel, unforgiving, indifferent, or powerless. And therefore, we are often critical of laments—and of sufferers who say such things—because they betray a mistaken understanding of God. And so we argue with the sufferer, carefully pointing out that God is not absent, nor is God cruel or indifferent to our pain. "You have it wrong," we say. "The trouble is with you and your understanding of God—not with God. You only think God is absent. God is always present. Don't you know that?"

And so we criticize the lament and the lamenter. The sufferer has one more thing to add to the burdens already present—a false perception of God. A sufferer who is already prone to self-blame for his or her troubles, now has one more put-down with which to contend.

We don't like them because they are hostile toward other people. The Bible teaches us to love one another, to be kind even to people we don't like. Jesus tells us even to love our enemies. Though none of us ever succeeds at that, we still know it is an ideal after which we should strive. Therefore, we are confused by lament psalms in which the psalmist vents a considerable amount of hostility toward enemies. Perhaps our enemies are ones who have caused our suffering, people who actually have hurt us in intentional or indirect ways. Maybe they are ones who are now gloating over our troubles, noting how our attempts to lead a good and pious life have failed to produce any rewards or prevent suffering. "All who see me mock at me, they make mouths at me, they wag their heads; 'He committed his cause to the Lord; let him deliver him, let him rescue him, for he delights in him!' " (Ps. 22:7-8). If God is just, if God wants to continue to attract followers, says the psalmist, God should treat faithful ones with more care. If good people continue to suffer like this while enemies of God flourish, the world will lose any sense of order and there will be no point in serving God. Some psalms are bitterly hostile and even curse other people, calling on God to destroy them with as much violence and pain as possible. Such psalms are difficult for us to reconcile with the admonitions about Christian love that we read in other parts of Scripture.

We don't like them because they make exaggerated claims for innocence. The psalmist does not always feel that the suffering is deserved. And in an effort to make that point, he sometimes gets carried away with claims for innocence, going on and on about what a great person he is, never doing anything wrong and certainly nothing that is bad enough to justify this kind of punishment. We cringe when we read such outrageous boasting about how good a person is. We know that we are all sinners and to claim to be otherwise is another evidence for bad theology on the part of the psalmist.

For these reasons, and no doubt for others, we have tended to be critical of biblical laments and of present-day sufferers who lapse into that kind of talk in reaction to their troubles. I have tried to present a fair case for why we dislike lament, but that is not the last word on the subject. Before we go on to talk about some ways in which laments might be helpful to us, it is important to make a distinction. The laments are not to be taken as an example of the way things are *supposed* to be. Rather, they are a description of the way things *are*. We should not study them as if they were source material for our doctrine of God or for ethical imperatives about how we should live with one another. When the lamenter says that God is hidden, the point is that it *seems* to the sufferer that God is hidden. We may teach that God is always present, but in the reality of the trauma of pain or grief, the sufferer cannot find God, and it is no help to such a person to stifle the lament and treat the problem as if it were a doctrinal formulation that must be corrected.

No one *wants* to think or feel like the writers of the lament psalms. They are not examples to be emulated. If there were no suffering in the world, there would be no need for lament. But given the world as it is, there may be times when we are in situations in which the laments help us to say what we already have been thinking, but weren't sure was permissible to admit. With this in mind, the laments may still be of significant value to us in times of trouble.

Laments can be helpful to sufferers

Laments allow honesty, realism, and integrity. Many persons are relieved to find the expression of negative feelings in the Bible. It provides some balance over against the constant pressure to pretend, to smile when they feel like crying, to say thanks to God when they are furious with God, to say they believe when they are full of doubts. Some people even begin to doubt their own sanity because it appears that everyone expects them to be going along as if things were normal and acceptable while on the inside their world has completely fallen apart.

Laments help keep the conversation with God open. How do you pray to God when you do not feel like praising, giving thanks, showing respect and dignity and the correct protocol? How do you address God if you think God is responsible for your trouble, or you doubt God's existence, or you are so angry about what God has done to you that you are afraid you would be struck with a lightning bolt if God ever found out?

A lament psalm is a prayer for times like that. It is a way to keep talking when we would prefer to draw away from God in doubt or disgust or anger or fear. At a time when our faith may be under trial, it is better to keep praying, and with honest prayers, than to stop praying because we can't pray the same sweet and positive words that we had spoken so easily in more pleasant days. The inclusion of such prayers in our Bible is a reminder that God encourages us to keep talking even when our theology is mixed up and we are angry and say things that we would never say if we were not so desperate.

Laments help break down our isolation in times of suffering. Often, in the midst of great trials, we think that we are the only persons in the world who have ever had to endure such awful things. No other Christian could ever have such terrifying thoughts about God, such hateful thoughts about other people, such a miserable feeling of depression. But then we discover these words in the Bible. Then we can say, "I am not the only one. David and Jeremiah and countless unknown persons of faith have had thoughts like mine. Perhaps there is hope for me, too. I am not alone. I am not crazy. Maybe I have not lost my faith after all."

A lament helps us to work through a process that is often necessary in times of suffering. A typical lament begins with a complaint addressed to God. It is important that it is addressed to God. It is not just purposeless whining into the wind, but it is coming to God, the one who can help. And it is also important that the complaint comes first, that we have the opportunity to say what hurts us, that we not be cut off too soon in the process by well-meaning comforters who think we are too full of self-pity or too hard on God or other people. Once we have had the opportunity to say our piece, then we will be better able to hear the good news that God has heard our pleas and will come to help. And so, the typical biblical lament begins with complaint but ends with praise. The one crying out of the depths has been heard and concludes the psalm with praise of a God who saves. The lament helps us remember the experience of God's people who cried to God for help in times of adversity and sang God's praise for the deliverance which came.

Jesus says the lament with us

One of the last words of Jesus from the cross is a lament, the opening lines of Psalm 22: "My God, my God, why hast thou forsaken me?" Those words of Jesus have been troublesome to Christians throughout the years. Why would Jesus say a thing like that? How could it be that he felt abandoned by God? If we have the urge to stifle lament even from an ordinary human being, we certainly don't want to hear such words from Jesus.

But surely Jesus suffered on the cross. Surely that was a terrible experience for him. The words of the psalm would have helped him pray what was on his mind and heart. Psalm 22 would have been an appropriate prayer from his Bible, from the book of Psalms.

Jesus was fully human. He knew what it was like to feel so alone and frightened that it was as if God had left. But Jesus is also God. And that means that God knows about our suffering. God has been there with us. When we cry out to God in our times of suffering, we know that we will be heard by one who truly knows what we have gone through. It is a great comfort for a sufferer to know the presence of an understanding and compassionate God, who not only invites our very human prayers but also knows what it is like to be in so much pain. God hears. God understands. God suffers with us. The lament is heard by one who has been there.

CHAPTER 3

Can Any Good Come from This?

Genesis 50:15-21

Suffering, by definition, is an unpleasant experience. We suffer for various reasons—physical illness, pain, grief, loneliness, self-doubt, fear, economic loss, confrontation with death, depression, and so on. No one wants to endure any of these things. We avoid them if at all possible. When they come, we often ask "Do I deserve this?" because their negative quality makes them seem like punishment. Or we cry out to God in our pain in the words of a lament. There is yet another biblical alternative, another possible way of understanding what suffering means. Perhaps, though it seems so awful, our suffering may actually be a blessing in disguise, an experience that will do us some good or bring some good to others. Is it possible that

31

something that looks so evil to the sufferer might actually be the vehicle for some greater good? Can any good come from this?

There are places in the Bible that suggest we may actually become better persons because of suffering. Eliphaz tells Job that he ought not to despise the chastening of the Almighty because the one whom God reproves will be happy (Job 5:17). The letter to the Hebrews (Chapter 12, quoting from Prov. 3:11-12) reminds us that God sometimes disciplines us just as a father disciplines his children. In Romans 5, Paul tells us that "suffering produces endurance, and endurance produces character, and character produces hope, and hope does not disappoint us" (vv. 3-4). Sometimes people can actually say, "Thanks, God, I needed that. Thanks for turning me around, helping me see what's important, getting my priorities straight, making me humble and dependent on you."

Other biblical texts speak of the blessings of suffering in a slightly different way. They, too, say that some good can come out of suffering, but it may be a benefit to other people, not the sufferer. The suffering servant in Isaiah 53 takes on the sins of other people and somehow eases their burdens. Jesus dies for us on the cross. He didn't need that for himself; it was for us. And now we too are told to pick up our cross and follow Jesus.

The end of the Joseph story is a lovely illustration of how the suffering of one can actually lead to the greater good of others (read Gen. 50:15-21). Jacob has died, and the brothers are afraid that Joseph will punish them for the evil they did to him. But he forgives them. He tells them that they meant to do him evil, but God meant it for good in order that many people would be saved at the time of famine. Joseph did not deserve to suffer the pain of being dragged away from home into slavery in a foreign land. That was an evil thing that his brothers did to him. God did not plan it or push them into it. They did it on their own. But, once they had done this to Joseph, God continued to work in the situation, making something good come from it. Because Joseph was in Egypt, many people were saved. An evil deed and great suffering on the part of Joseph became the means to something good. Good can come from situations that seem terrible, totally negative, with no possible redeeming value.

So there are some places in the Bible which give a positive response to the question of the sufferer: "Can any good come from this?" Let us think in more depth about the possibility that our suffering, as bad as it seems, may have some value for either ourselves or others.

We move beyond suffering as punishment

This view is an advance over a narrow view of retribution that tries to identify every example of suffering as the result of some specific sin. It diverts our attention away from the cause of the suffering and tries to focus our attention on the future.

Where do we go from here? Can some good come out of this awful mess that we are in? No matter what caused it—our own sins, God's doing, the freedom of other human beings to hurt us, just plain bad luck—there is the possibility that God can use it for some greater good. God is still working for us. No experience is so bad, no suffering so acute, no torment so severe, that God cannot bring some good out of it.

Understanding comes later

At the moment of suffering, it is impossible to see how such unpleasantness could ever lead to anything good. A sufferer will probably be angry if you even suggest such a possibility. As Joseph was being dragged off from his home and family to the unknown of faraway Egypt, there was no way that he could have known that some day many would be saved because the jealousy of his brothers had exiled him to Egypt. Only at the end of many years, as he looked back over an intricate chain of events, was Joseph able to see God's hand in all of this and realize that something had been gained because of his suffering.

Hindsight is a wonderful thing. The farther we are removed from our suffering, the more likely we are to accept the possibility that good can come from it. This has been the testimony of countless Christians who have been convinced that they were

34

better people and could be better helpers to others because of their own suffering. For example, groups of those who have had similar kinds of suffering come together for mutual support, such as AA, hospice units for the dying, or groups of single parents or parents who have suffered the death of a child. Those who have been there before, who have endured a similar suffering, are those most likely to be helpful.

Finding something positive in our affliction

"Can any good come from this?" The person of faith is much more likely to answer yes to this question. People who believe in a good God try very hard to find evidence of God at work in the world. In times of severe suffering, that evidence is more difficult to find. But people keep looking and hoping, desperately seeking some benefit that could make the present pain tolerable. If we can see that there is some meaning to it all, it is much easier to bear.

I met a woman who had suffered a chronic illness for over 20 of her 46 years. She was almost constantly in pain. She spent about half her life in the hospital, and most of her time at home was spent in bed. I knew she was a Christian and must have had some way of reconciling her terrible experiences with her belief in a good God. How did she come to terms with her own suffering? She told me she did not believe she deserved her suffering. She dismissed that answer a long time ago. She was not that bad and God was not that cruel for such a thing to be possible. Sometimes she found some comfort in the lament, in the freedom to lay her troubles before God, to confront God with her pain and doubts and anger and fear. But most of all, she found comfort in the belief that some good might come to others because of her illness.

She tried to make herself available to other sufferers, to share with them how she had endured. And she sometimes met with doctors and ministers to give them feedback from one who was suffering, so that they might understand how the sufferer perceives what doctors and ministers say and do. But, for her, the most important example of her belief that her suffering had some value had to do with her children. She had two teenagers—a boy and a girl. She was convinced that they were better people—less selfish, more compassionate, more able to bring comfort to other people—because of living with her through all her suffering. That idea was a great source of strength to her. Her suffering was not meaningless.

Do not interpret someone else's suffering for them

The woman had come to the conclusion, on her own, with considerable hindsight, with a great need to find value in her suffering, and perhaps with the help of some Bible passages, that her suffering could accomplish some greater good. Since it was her idea and since it seemed to help her, it was probably true. Her faith helped to make it true. Her children are evidence that it is true. Who can argue, or who would want to?

But it would not be wise for you or me or anyone else to suggest this interpretation to another person in the midst of great suffering. Consider these situations: A family has just heard that their youngest daughter was killed in an automobile accident. Who would face that family and say that God has some greater purpose in mind? A 35-year-old mother of four has just received the diagnosis of terminal cancer. Only a terribly insensitive person would be quick to volunteer the possibility that this might make her a better person or bring the family together or move her closer to God. If it is ever possible to say such things—and it may never be—it will only be with more distance from the immediate pain, and it will only be valid if the sufferer can honestly accept the interpretation.

There may be value that comes from our suffering. Many believers have attested to that. But it does not always happen. Sometimes the suffering is so severe that there seems to be no redeeming value, even with years of hindsight and an impassioned desire to find meaning. Not all suffering will yield a positive answer to the question, "Can any good come from this?" Sometimes the mystery remains.

God uses Jesus' death on the cross for a greater purpose

Perhaps this way of thinking about meaning in suffering can shed some light on how we think about Jesus' crucifixion. The suffering of Jesus, hanging there in great pain, dying the death of a criminal, being humiliated by every passerby, was a terrible thing. How could any good have ever come from such an event? It was an awful example of what human beings are like, the kind of evil they do to one another, the rejection of even the one who comes with love, the one whom God sent. You would think that would be just one more condemnation of the rotten world in which we live and a reminder that we are all sinners who deserve to be punished for our treatment of Jesus. But the crucifixion is not the end. That most awful of events becomes the means of salvation, the way God chose to reach out to the world and save it.

Though human beings, out of evil motives, wanted to kill Jesus, God meant it for good—just as Joseph's brothers meant to do evil to him, but God meant it for good. At the moment of his death Jesus' followers could see no value in this. It seemed like the end. They scattered in fear and disillusionment. The promise was destroyed. It was only with hindsight, after the resurrection, after they knew they were forgiven and that death had been conquered and Jesus really was the Messiah, that they were able to see that Jesus' death had value. He died for us, and by his blood we are saved. That most awful of days is now called Good Friday, and we wear the cross around our necks and hang it in our churches. That symbol of a vicious and terrible form of execution has become a sign of God's redemption of the world.

God can make good come out of our suffering. It does not matter where the suffering comes from—out of our own doing or the evil deeds of others or some hidden mystery. The important point is that God does not abandon us in our suffering. There is nothing that can happen to us, to our loved ones, or to our world that is so bad that it can separate us from the love of God or make it impossible for God's healing power to have its effect.

"Can any good come from this?" Maybe. At least we know that God is still at work in our lives, and suffering never has the last word.

CHAPTER 4

Why Do My Friends Condemn Me?

Job 6:14-27

A sufferer often feels like an outcast, one whom people avoid and even condemn. A time when a person needs friendship, a comforting word, the warm presence of another human being is often the very time when that seems to be most distant. "No one comes to see me anymore." "My friends have forgotten about me." "They seem nervous when they are here. I almost am relieved when they leave." "Are they afraid of me?" "They talk as if they blame me for my own trouble." Sufferers often have had reactions like this when they have felt let down by even their close friends and relatives. And they ask, "Why do my friends condemn me?"

Job had similar experiences with the friends who came to see him. Eliphaz and Bildad and Zophar made an appointment to come together to be with Job and try to bring him some comfort. They were so moved by his appearance when they first saw him that they wept for him. They sat with him silently for a week, letting him know their care and concern. Finally Job broke the silence with a bitter lament, wishing that he had never been born, but, since it was too late to change that, hoping that he would die quickly and be out of his misery.

Then one of the three friends, Eliphaz, began to talk to Job. He tried to be gentle with him. He raised some possible explanations for Job's troubles. God was fair and would not do this to Job without some reason, Eliphaz maintained. Perhaps Job really had committed some sin which needed to be examined and confessed and forgiven. After all, even good people like Job were guilty of sin, so there might have been some problem area which Job had not taken care of as he should. God would bring him through this safely, Eliphaz promised. Perhaps Job would even be a better person for having endured this suffering. "Happy is the man whom God reproves" (Job 5:17a).

On the surface, this sounds harmless enough, perhaps even helpful. Eliphaz brought to Job's attention many of the traditional ways in which religious people understand the origin and purpose of suffering. We have already looked at some of these earlier in this book.

But Job's response was far from grateful. He did not thank Eliphaz and the others for coming. He did not tell them that their words helped him. Rather, he became angry and complained that they were not good comforters. They let him down. They condemned rather than helped. Listen to some of Job's words: "He who withholds kindness from a friend forsakes the fear of the Almighty. My brethren are treacherous as a torrent-bed, as freshets that pass away, which are dark with ice, and where the snow hides itself. In time of heat they disappear; when it is hot, they vanish from their place" (6:14-17). Later Job said, "Lo, my eye has seen all this, my ear has heard and understood it. What you know, I also know: I am not inferior to you" (13:1-2).

Something went wrong. Job's friends came to help Job in his time of sorrow. They tried the same approach they had used before with other sufferers. But they got a hostile reaction. Job thought he was condemned, and the counselors thought they were insulted. Why do sufferers so often feel abandoned and blamed at times of suffering? Why do well-intentioned comforters often say and do things that bring about this reaction in the one who needs comfort? Let us think about some possible reasons for this.

Locked into ideas of retribution

We all want the world to be fair. Certainly we want God to act toward the world with justice, not arbitrarily bringing evil to both good people and bad people alike. God should act according to some recognizable plan so that we can make sense out of the world. When innocent people suffer and wicked people prosper, we have trouble understanding. Often we would rather change our estimate of the one who is suffering than give up the idea that God is fair and life is fair and people get what they deserve.

This means that sometimes we would rather feel guilty than live with a sense of meaninglessness. Sufferers often condemn themselves, because at least that makes some sense out of their troubles. And the process is similar with those who bring comfort. Job's friends knew that Job was a good man, but they also believed that God was just and would never do such awful things to someone without a good reason. So, something had to give. And, in the minds of Job's friends, what had to yield was their estimate of Job's character. He must not have been as good a person as they had thought he was. There must have been some sin hiding in his past. No one is perfect, not even Job. At the least, Job could have benefited from discipline in order to smooth off the rough spots (perhaps he needed a little more humility) and make him an even better person.

In a subtle way, Job's counselors began to condemn Job in order to protect their ideas about God's justice at work in the world. It is too scary to give up that sense of order and coherence. Better to change our view of Job than to abandon a way of understanding suffering that has been around for a long, long time.

So Job, like many sufferers, felt condemned—as if his suffering were his own fault, as if he had brought it on himself, as if he could have done something to prevent it or acted differently once it came. And since the sufferer is also desperately seeking for some sense of meaning, he or she may accept the condemnation, preferring guilt to meaninglessness.

No answers to the sufferer's questions

A sufferer is always asking, *Why?* "Why is this happening to me?" "Why me and not someone else?" "Why does God let such things happen in the world if God really loves us?" "Why do my old friends and acquaintances now turn away from me in disgust?" "Why did my child or spouse die?"

We anticipate the questions the sufferer will ask and we know we have no answers. And, therefore, we stay away, we forget to call on the phone, we are too busy to take the time to listen to that tale of woe one more time. No one wants to feel stupid. No one wants to admit helplessness in the face of human misery. We wish we could say or do something that would make the suffering go away or give it meaning or help change the sufferer's attitude—but we cannot. We feel inadequate and helpless and ignorant, and we stay away from the sufferer because the questions he or she will ask us are too hard to answer.

And so the sufferer is left without our presence, which might be of some help, because we fear our inability to deal with the questions. Most sufferers know we cannot give them easy answers. They ask their hard questions, to be sure, but they don't really expect us to answer them. They just want us to listen to them, to know something about how hard it is for them, to let them know that we care. But our fear of saying the wrong thing or saying nothing keeps us from being there with the sufferer. And the sufferer feels condemned, betrayed by former friends.

"They are disappointed because they were confident; they come thither and are confounded. Such you have now become to me; you see my calamity, and are afraid" (Job 6:20-21).

Interpreting lament as unbelief

Sometimes comforters are drawn into arguments with a sufferer. That certainly happened with Job and his friends. A person in trouble may say things for which he or she would not wish to be accountable at a later time. Earlier we talked about some of the objections to lament, some of the reasons we suppress them. We see them as bad psychology and bad theology. We tend to argue with the words of the sufferer rather than identifying with the pain which brought on such words. "My God, why have you forsaken me?" is not a cry that demonstrates lack of faith. On the contrary, it shows an enormous amount of faith, a willingness to come to God even with our negative feelings, even when we are angry with God or doubtful of God's existence. To carry on and pray to God honestly at a time like that is a strong assertion of faith. And we ought not to argue about a person's theology in a prayer that is spoken out of the depths.

Sometimes the sufferer feels condemned because, after daring to be open and honest about the feelings and thoughts that are pressing in on mind and heart, a friend responds with a reprimand: "Don't think that. God is not like that. You have it wrong. You must get your thinking straight."

Job said to his counselors, "How forceful are honest words! But what does reproof from you reprove? Do you think that you can reprove words, when the speech of a despairing man is wind?" (Job 6:25-26).

Suffering often brings out the worst in people

It is no wonder that comforters sometimes speak a condemning word to sufferers. A person like Job is not easy to talk to. You try to help the person. You share your best insights about meaning in suffering. You take time away from family and work to be with the person, maybe even losing part of your paycheck to spend the week with him or her. And what do you get but a barrage of insults about how condemning you are and how your counsel is worthless and how it would be better for everyone if you would just shut up. After listening to a tirade like that, it is rather difficult to keep cool and not respond in anger.

Suffering often brings out the worst in people. When the going gets rough, most of us do not become patient saints. More likely, suffering leads to self-centeredness, crankiness, and anger toward God and other human beings (including the bearer of comfort). Sufferers are not very lovable. It is hard to hang in there with a sufferer. It is no wonder we sometimes slip in a word of condemnation, however indirect. There is usually something to criticize in the behavior of a typical sufferer. Even if we don't actually condemn, the sufferer will probably think that is what we are doing.

God loves sufferers

Sufferers do not feel people are responding properly to their pain. It is hard to find comfort from another human being, someone who totally understands and truly cares and will not condemn.

From the perspective of one who tries to bring consolation, it is very hard to be a comforter. Though we want to help, we discover that we are protecting ourselves and our ideas, feeling uncomfortable about our inability to know what to say or do, turned off by the anger and bitterness of the one who is suffering.

Human comforters will always be inadequate. Sufferers know that. Comforters do too. But the God revealed in Jesus Christ loves even the unlovable, the outcast, the hateful one, even the unbeliever. Sufferers can look beyond the feeble efforts of friends to bring comfort and know there is a God who does not condemn or hide from their pain. And the comforter can try to help the sufferer see beyond our imperfect human response to suffering to the image of a God who has loved us enough to die for us. That is the God that we can come to in time of trouble—and we will not be turned away empty.

CHAPTER 5

Why Doesn't God Do Something?

Genesis 6:5-8

In times of suffering, religious people turn to God for help. Even if other human beings let us down, even if the whole world seems to turn against us, even if the best of medical science offers no hope, at least we can turn to God. We have been taught that God cares about us and has the power to help us. God has promised to hear the cries of those in distress. Jesus tells us to come knocking on the door, asking and seeking, and we shall find what we are looking for.

We have learned that God is in charge of the world. Whatever God wants, God gets. God has the power. If God wants to do something, no one or nothing is going to stop him.

This belief in God's power can cause us great anguish in times of suffering. If God can do something to take away the misery of the world, then why doesn't he do it? How can God sit idly by while innocent people suffer? If we were God, we imagine, *we* would do something about the pain of the world and not let it continue like this. If God is powerful enough to prevent misery, but does not do it, does that mean that there is some doubt about God's mercy and justice? Is God less caring than we humans? Why doesn't God do something?

The question of suffering raises for us this difficult question about God's power as over against God's mercy. We want a God who has both attributes. As long as everything goes well for us and we do not suffer excessively (we lead reasonably prosperous and pleasant lives, and we don't come too close to other people's suffering), then we are able to keep these two characteristics of God in balance. God is both merciful and powerful. God cares for the hurting of the world and does something about it.

But when the innocent suffer, when children and old people are victimized by the powerful and greedy, when evil governments defeat good ones, and rare and terrible diseases afflict the wrong persons, then we have a hard time believing in a God who is both good and powerful. "Why doesn't God do something?" we ask. Is it because God does not care enough to do something? Is God unmoved by what he sees? Or is it perhaps that God is unable to do anything, lacking the power to prevent or remove the suffering?

If we must choose between one of these alternatives—and it is at times of suffering that we are most likely to feel we are being forced into one or the other—which is better? Which is least disturbing? If we must choose to give up a belief in God's mercy or a belief in God's power, which would be easier to handle?

What if God is not merciful?

This is probably the most frightening thought of all. If the God that is the creator and sustainer of the world is not predisposed to think kindly toward human beings, then we are indeed in a hopeless situation. We are completely at the mercy of arbitrary forces that can do whatever they want to us, and there is no one to defend us. It would be very difficult to love and trust a God who has power but no mercy.

Job was beginning to think about God like that. Job had no doubt that God had power. To Job, it was part of the definition of God that God can do whatever he wants just because he is God. Therefore, as far as Job was concerned, whatever happened in the world was God's doing. Nothing could happen without God willing it. When disasters struck Job, there was no doubt that God had caused them (or as some people say in trying to relieve the pressure a little, God "allowed" them). God had taken Job's children, wiped out his property, and given him an awful disease. If there had been some reason for it, perhaps Job could still believe in a God who has both power *and* mercy. But Job could not find a reason. His friends came around to help him find an explanation, but they only made matters worse. Something had to give—either the belief in God's power or the belief in God's justice. For Job, the first to go was his belief in God's goodness and mercy and justice. And so Job accused God of being unfair, cruel, and uncaring—but still powerful.

It is a terrible crisis of faith when you still believe in God's power but you are beginning to doubt that God cares.

Many times, when disasters come to people they say, "It must have been God's will." A little girl on her tricycle is run over by a speeding car, and her parents say, "It must have been God's will." A little boy happens to witness a kidnapping, so he too is dragged away and later murdered. Months later, when the body is found and the parents try to make some sense out of the tragedy, they speak about God's purpose in causing (or "allowing") all of this to happen. If God plans and controls all the events that take place on this earth, if God really has that kind of power, then it is rather hard to continue to believe in a God of mercy.

Many contemporary Jews have a hard time believing in a God who is both powerful and merciful after the experience of the Holocaust, in World War II, when six million Jews were slaughtered. If

God has power, he must not have any compassion to allow such an awful thing to happen.

If we insist that God is a God of power, that everything that happens is in God's control and was willed by him, then we cannot help but wonder about the goodness of God.

What if God is not all-powerful?

If it is terrible to contemplate a God who is powerful but not obviously merciful, is it any more comforting to imagine a God who is filled with compassion but has limited power? If one or the other must give in the tension of actual suffering, is it better to give up a little on our notions of God's power? Which way should we lean?

Maybe there are some things that God cannot change or control—at least for the time being. For some people, that thought must be almost as terrifying as the thought that God is not merciful. If God is not in charge, if God cannot control what happens, if the world is lurching out of control in a meaningless meandering and our own lives are a succession of undirected episodes in which we are simply either lucky or unlucky, then it seems there is no place to turn for help. If God has no control, no power to help us, then what are we to do but to stick it out in a grim stoic acquiescence to the fates?

There are many biblical passages which imply limitations to God's power. God created a world that had some order to it. It is a complex world of complicated balances and interconnections. What happens in one part of the creation has its effects in other parts. Once the world was made, God was somewhat limited in what could be done with it. Cause-and-effect relationships are at work that cannot be removed or suspended without causing utter chaos for someone or something somewhere else in the world. For example, the law of gravity cannot be suspended in one part of the creation without having dire effects elsewhere.

For some reason God created humans with the freedom to trust or rebel. Conceivably God could have created creatures with no possibility of rebellion, who would always know God's will and never fail to comply with it. How much simpler life would have been for God (if not for those creatures). But as long as the world remains a place in which human beings are given the freedom to act in defiance of God, it will be a world in which God does not have the complete control over what is happening. We cannot say that God is responsible for everything that happens. As long as humans are allowed to hurt themselves and each other, God does not have that kind of power. At one point God was not sure he had done the right thing in making the world that way. In the events leading up to the flood, we read: "The Lord saw that the wickedness of man was great in the earth, and that every imagination of the thoughts of his heart was only evil continually. And the Lord was sorry that he had made man on the earth, and it grieved him to his heart" (Gen. 6:5-6).

This is not the picture of a God who has complete power over everything. Human beings had been doing other than what God wanted. They were hurting each other, and it grieved God to the heart to see what humans were doing to the beautiful creation that had been given to them. There is, however, compassion in this picture of God. God suffers with the creation. God cannot make human beings live the way that they should; he can only suffer with them. The world had not turned out the way that it should, so God pondered destroying it. What God truly wanted was a world that responded in love and obedience, that trusted God and did not fret and worry about things that God will take care of. Just like human beings, God could not make others love him. God was tempted to forget about this experiment with human beings and wipe out the world completely, but later changed his mind, started over with Noah and his family, and vowed (with the rainbow as sign) never again to bring a flood to destroy the earth.

What if God is merciful, but not all-powerful? Is that a more comforting word than the possibility that God is all powerful but not merciful? I think so. At least it makes it possible to believe in a God who is *good*, so I do not have to blame God for all the bad things that are happening. Perhaps they are not caused by God at all and are not even desired by God. Perhaps God is grieved and pained when looking on the suffering of the world. Just to know that can be a comforting word for a sufferer. Better to have a God who cares, but, for the moment at least, cannot remove our suffering, than to have a God who could remove our suffering if desired, but remains cold and indifferent to our pain.

But we must be careful not to let go of too much of God's power. In our present world, for whatever reason, there may be limitations on God's power. But that is not the way it will always be. Suffering does not have the last word. Life is not without meaning. God does have the final say, though it may not be until the next world that God's will is accomplished in its fullness.

"Why doesn't God do something?" That is the cry of the sufferer who believes that God has the power to help but does not see the help forthcoming.

In Christ, God removes forever doubts about his mercy

Our experiences leave us baffled. In the absence of relief from our suffering, we might be tempted to believe that God does not love us, that God is not moved by our plight. But any doubt about that should be removed by the sacrifice of Jesus Christ on the cross. Here is God coming to us in weakness, like our own weakness. God's power is put aside. The crucifixion is allowed to continue. Those who plot the terrible deed are not struck dead. God does not intervene. God's power is withheld that we may know once and for all that the God who made the world is more interested in convincing us of how much we are loved than in demonstrating power. Too many people know that God is powerful, but they do not know how much God grieves over the hurts and sufferings of his people. On the cross, God humbled himself to be like us and bear our sorrow. God does not coerce us, but wants to show us that he is worthy of our trust and devotion.

There will be victory, of course. The suffering of the moment is not forever. God is not without power. God raised Jesus from the dead. Death had no power over him. There is nothing in all creation or anywhere else that can compete with the power of God. Though God's power to remove the present pain seems limited, there is no question about God's ultimate power finally to defeat all evil. It may not come within this life. But it will come—as at that first Easter morn—either by his coming again or, if we die before that (which is probably more likely), through the promise of eternal life.

Why doesn't God do something? God has done something. He has sent us Jesus Christ, who suffered and died for us. And he will do more, some day making complete the victory which was begun on that first Easter.

CHAPTER 6

Whose Fault Is It?

Romans 8:31-39

Sufferers have a powerful compulsion to fix the blame. Someone must be at fault. Such an awful experience as suffering could not happen by accident. There must be a meaning. One of the ways in which we try to make sense out of our suffering is to assign blame. "Whose fault is it?" we ask. If we can know that, then the world does not seem quite so chaotic and out of control. If we can get some idea who has caused our suffering, we can begin to gain some control over our lives and ease the feeling of being swept along by terrible, unpredictable, and completely arbitrary forces. There appears to be some comfort in naming the source of our troubles. At the same time, such speculation can also be very disturbing to the sufferer.

Whose fault is it? There really aren't that many possibilities. I can think of four: God, other people, myself, or the devil. Let us look at each of these one at a time.

God is the source of our suffering

God is supposed to be in charge of the world. Perhaps then, God has brought our suffering. Does God bring bad things to us as well as good things? This is a hard question to ask. After Job had lost all his wealth and all his children had died, he hunched up his shoulders, took a deep breath and said, "Naked I came from my mother's womb, and naked shall I return; the Lord gave, and the Lord has taken away; blessed be the name of the Lord" (Job 1:21). Later, after a terrible skin disease was added to the woes already dumped on him, Job argued with his wife, "Shall we receive good at the hand of God, and shall we not receive evil?" (Job 2:10b). Job assumed that all comes from God, both good and evil, because God is God and controls the world. We discussed in the previous chapter some of the problems we have when we accent God's power to the point of making it difficult to see evidence of God's mercy.

Certainly God has some responsibility for the suffering of the world. He did create the world, and it is only by God's will that it continues to exist in its present state. Surely God could bring the suffering to an end, though he might have to bring the world to an end in order to do it. Whether or not we can assign blame to God for our individual experiences of suffering, at least God is responsible in a general way for creating and allowing to continue a world in which humans are often required to suffer.

Many times the Bible talks about God bringing suffering to people as a punishment for their sins. So, in a sense, God is responsible for some suffering because God plays the role of a judge who brings good and evil to people as they deserve. The Bible makes it clear, however, that God never wants to punish, that God would always prefer to hold back unpleasantness and takes no delight in the death or hurt of anyone. Nevertheless, God does sometimes bring suffering when provoked by our sin or when there is some greater good in mind (as we discussed earlier in regard to the question "Can any good come from this?").

So, one possible answer to our question, "Whose fault is it?" is God.

Other people may cause our suffering

Our suffering could be the result of sins committed by people who lived before us, or sins of people who do not even know who we are, or sins of people who in a more direct way have caused our pain.

Maybe the ones to blame are our ancestors, the ones who left the world in such a horrible state for the present generation. It is not uncommon to blame fathers and mothers for our own troubles, and in many cases, it is at least partly justified. We Christians, in fact, trace our problems all the way back to our first parents, Adam and Eve. In several places in the Bible (including Exod. 34:6-7), we read that the sins of the fathers are to be passed on to the third and fourth generation of those who hate the Lord. Previous generations have stolen land from Native Americans, held Black people as slaves, polluted the landscape and the air and water, fought "wars to end all wars" that actually prepared the way for future wars, invented ever new and more terrible weapons, and all of us have suffered and will suffer because of that legacy. In a more personal way, we inherit the genes and the personality problems of our more immediate ancestors, some of which might predispose us toward certain kinds of suffering. Many young persons who have been through psychological counseling have, at least for a time, fixed much of the blame for their suffering on their parents: "My mother was too smothering with her love" "My father was too demanding in his discipline."

We may be suffering because of complex interconnections that exist in a society and world like ours. Congress hacks off a few million dollars from the budget, and women and children must bear extra suffering. Politicians for whom we never voted, who do not know us at all, make decisions that may cause us a great amount of suffering. We may fix the blame for our suffering even on those who have no direct personal connection with us at all.

Of course, we also have enemies at close range. There are people who hurt us, intentionally or not, whom we can see and know. The writers of the psalms often talk about enemies who have hurt them directly, who have not brought proper comfort, or who have gloated about their misfortunes. People do hurt other people. And often sufferers lash out at others, trying to find someone to blame, sometimes realistically and sometimes out of a kind of paranoia fueled by the suffering. We may even get to the point of finding scapegoats, someone on whom we can project the fault so that we can make sense out of it: "If the doctor had caught it sooner." "If only my boss was not so picky and arrogant." "If only my spouse was more understanding." "If only the Russians would quit stirring up trouble all over the world."

Other people do hurt us and cause suffering — even those who lived before us or who don't know us but make decisions which affect us. Sometimes, however, our need to find enemies in order to help explain suffering drives us to unrealistic and hostile attitudes toward imagined enemies.

Perhaps we cause our own suffering

Earlier in this book we talked about the question, "Do I deserve this?" It is not uncommon for people to blame themselves for their suffering. When searching around for the guilty party, many do not look any farther than themselves. "Perhaps God is punishing me for some sin," they think. "Maybe God has nothing to do with it, but it is still my fault." "Maybe I should have done something differently." "Maybe if I had not had so much stress in my life." "Maybe if I had not lost my temper." "Maybe if I had tried harder to get along with my spouse and children." "Maybe if I had had enough will power to quit smoking those cigarettes."

Again, this can be realistic and helpful, giving some sense to our suffering, providing some hints about how to avoid similar experiences of suffering in the future. But it can also be futile and conducive to unnecessary guilt. Unfortunately, many would rather blame themselves than not blame anyone at all. The obsession with fixing blame is strong because of our need to rationalize our suffering, and so we would rather live with guilt than with meaninglessness. Forgiveness is often hard to accept, because our guilt is serving a function in providing meaning for our suffering.

Maybe we should blame the devil

Is there anyone to blame besides God and human beings? Could there be some hostile evil forces, in between God and humans, more powerful than human beings, but no match for God? Sometimes, when trying to assign blame for suffering, we are uncomfortable in blaming God *or* human beings *or* ourselves. We do not want to think of a good God bringing such horrible events. They seem too enormous and hideous for humans to think up all by themselves. And surely we do not think that we are such horrible sinners that we would ever deserve such violent retribution. It would be good if we could blame someone else, some evil force, something neither God nor human that means to do us harm.

In several places the Bible speaks of such an evil force in the world. There is a sudden appearance of the snake in the Garden of Eden, abruptly throwing a shadow of gloom over the beauty of the creation. Some Old Testament poetry speaks of God engaging in battle with dragons, like Rahab and Leviathan, who live in the sea. Late Old Testament books talk about a heavenly being called Satan who is determined to test and push human beings to the breaking point so that they will lose their faith in God. The New Testament speaks about demons and evil spirits that enter into humans and cause physical and psychological suffering. The devil is personified as the prince of demons, the one in charge of all these hostile forces acting against God and humanity and causing many of the trials and tribulations of life.

What are we to make of all this? Many modern people have a hard time talking about such things. We look for medical, chemical, sociological, and psychological explanations for things that in ancient days may have been understood as the presence of evil forces in the universe. But this remains as one of the biblical possibilities in our search for whom to blame for our suffering. Perhaps the devil did it to us.

It can be helpful to put the blame someplace else than on God or ourselves. It is easier to come to God seeking comfort if we do not think God has caused our trouble. Then God is not the judge, the adversary, the prosecuting attorney. Instead God is on our side in our battle against evil and we can go to God seeking help against a common enemy. Since we do not have to blame ourselves, we can be relieved of unnecessary guilt. The problem, of course, is that we should not be too quick to excuse ourselves from guilt which may be realistic and appropriate. Rather than blame the devil, perhaps we should accept our own responsibility, in at least some examples of suffering.

So in our search for meaning in a time of suffering we ask, "Whose fault is it?" There are at least these four possibilities: God, other people, myself, the devil—or some complicated mix of two or more of them. Not every example of suffering will originate from the same source; each example must be looked at by itself. Though it may be our fault in one case, it may be someone else's in another. We should never let ourselves get locked into a simplistic answer that treats every suffering experience as if it were the same as every other one.

A biblical word of encouragement

If our inclination is to blame God, we are reminded that God is not our enemy. God always wants what is best for us. Any doubts about God's good intentions for the world have been forever settled in the suffering and death of Jesus Christ. In Jesus we have a God who goes to the greatest lengths possible to demonstrate love, concern, and mercy toward human beings. God would rather suffer with us than to punish us for our sins.

The bottom line.

If other people have caused us suffering, it is comforting to know that God will take care of that. In anger and pain, we may cry out to God in a curse, hoping God will bring some awful vengeance on our tormentors. But even as we say those awful things, we are relieved that God will take our words with a grain of salt, that God will execute justice with mercy. " 'Vengeance is mine, I will repay,' says the Lord" (Rom. 12:19). It is good to be able to leave it that way. Let God bring the final vindication. Let God sort out our hatred which may be justified from that which is projected out of frustration and a need to find a scapegoat. God is best capable of separating the wheat from the chaff.

If we have brought on our own suffering, we know that we can be forgiven. God can help us change. God can even teach us through the errors of the past so that we may be better equipped for life's tribulations as we continue our pilgrimage through life.

If the devil or some other personification of evil forces seeks to hurt us, it is good to know that there is no one or no thing strong enough to hurt us. "If God is for us, who is against us? . . . For I am sure that neither death, nor life, nor angels, nor principalities, nor things present, nor things to come, nor powers, nor height, nor depth, nor anything else in all creation, will be able to separate us from the love of God in Christ Jesus our Lord" (Rom. 8:31, 38-39).

Finally, we are relieved even from the necessity of finding fault, assigning blame. Perhaps there is no one to blame. After we have looked at all of the possibilities, we may conclude that none of them explains our own suffering. It is no one's fault; it makes no sense. If we truly trust in God, we can live even without an answer to our question, "Whose fault is it?" We can even give up on the question and live with the mystery, knowing that God has promised to be with us and to take care of that which we cannot yet fully understand. All of our questions fade into proper perspective in the knowledge and presence of a God like that.

CHAPTER 7

Is There
Any Hope?

1 Corinthians 15:12-26

Sufferers often feel that there is no way out of their suffering. They feel as if they are at the bottom of a pit with no way to climb out, locked in a room with no exit, or stranded in the middle of a long tunnel with no glimmer of light to indicate an opening at the end. If only there were some hope, something to look forward to, some way of escape, some assurance that the present state is not going to last forever. So the sufferer cries out, "Is there any hope? Or am I doomed always to feel exactly the way I feel right now?"

Let us look at some of the hopes that sustain people during times of suffering.

Restoration and deliverance in this life

Most sufferers want the suffering to go away. And they want it to happen as soon as possible, if not immediately. If they are sick and in pain, they want to be well. They want the broken family relationships to be restored. They want the sentence of death pronounced by the doctor to be postponed—forever, if possible. They want depression to be replaced with a feeling of peace, and hostility to be pushed aside by love. They want the suffering of this life to end. That is the first thing a sufferer hopes for.

We turn on the TV and the hucksters of mass-media religion promise us that we can indeed have our suffering removed. All we need to do is say our prayers with the right intensity, have enough faith, trust the particular preacher whose show we are watching, and perhaps send a little money so that the good work of healing can continue to reach homes all over the country. One after another, examples of former sufferers are paraded before us, one outdoing the other to see who can smile the biggest smile as they tell us how God acted to take away their trouble.

How much can we hope for in this life? Surely, in most cases, the suffering does go away. People do get well. We work through the unpleasant experiences of grief, separation, loneliness, and depression, and often we are stronger for our ordeal. Sometimes, though not often, cures that look like miracles occur, where a pessimistic prognosis turns out to be incorrect.

But sometimes relief from suffering does *not* come. No matter how much faith we have, we all will die some day. No matter how tenaciously we implore God to heal our loved one from terminal cancer, the odds are overwhelmingly on the side of the doctor's gloomy prediction. Often people are doubly troubled when their prayers seemingly are not answered. They asked for their suffering to be removed, but that did not happen. Now they continue to suffer, with the added burden of wondering if their prayer was not answered because they just didn't have enough faith.

The letdown can make our suffering even greater if we had set our hopes too high, if we had looked for removal of all suffering within this life. If our faith is tied to visible evidence of God jumping to answer our prayers by removing our suffering, then we are indeed on shaky ground. Every time we get a no to our prayers we will be in a crisis of faith.

We all know the stories of Jesus' healing of the sick and suffering of his day. And we hope it could be like that for us, too. But sometimes the biblical characters did not receive what they asked for in prayer. David prayed that the child born to him and Bathsheba would be allowed to live, but the child died (2 Sam. 12:15b-23). Moses, the great hero who had delivered Israel from bondage in Egypt and had led them through the wilderness for 40 years, pleaded with God to allow him to go over into the promised land, but God said no (Deut. 3:23-27). Three times Paul begged God to remove his thorn in the flesh. Whatever that thorn was, it was obviously a problem for Paul and possibly an impediment to the work he was doing on behalf of the church. But God said no. "My grace is sufficient for you, for my power is made perfect in weakness" (2 Cor. 12:9).

The New Testament makes it clear that Christians will not be able to avoid all suffering. In some ways, we may even suffer more than others, because of our Christian faith. We are told to pick up our crosses and follow Christ—hardly an assurance that being a Christian will make life easier with less hardships and suffering than befall other human beings.

We cannot promise people that the suffering will go away—not in this life, anyway. It may happen, but it may not. The loved one may die. The depression may seem to last forever. The chronic pain will not yield to pain killers. The broken family will not be reconciled. But we ought not to condemn ourselves one more time because our fervent prayer has not been answered. Even Moses, David, and Paul had to deal with no's from God. Should we expect better treatment than they?

If, in fact, the suffering will not go away—at least for awhile—for what else can we hope while the suffering remains?

The support of other human beings

Sufferers tend to feel lonely and isolated. They feel sorry for themselves, as if no one in the world has ever had to bear such a burden. And they hope for someone to listen to them, to support them, to give strength and a sense of community. At times of suffering, we hope for a shoulder to cry on, someone to understand, someone to weep with us. The presence of such human comfort helps make the present suffering more bearable.

That may sound like a modest hope, but it is important, and it is not always easy to find. As we mentioned earlier, often a sufferer feels condemned. Even close friends seem to have turned away, and it is hard to find a sympathetic ear. The behavior of sufferers makes them hard to love. Their insistence on answers from us makes us feel stupid and inadequate in our feeble efforts to bring comfort. It is not easy to be a comforter to a sufferer. Job had hoped that at least he could get some human comfort in his time of suffering, but it did not work out very well. He felt betrayed and let down by his friends.

We should be able to fulfill this hope of the sufferer. The church should be a place for the mutual consolation of sufferers. Though we cannot promise that a person will have suffering removed, we should be able to promise that a person will have the support of fellow Christians. And by demonstrating that human beings love and support the sufferer, we are also conveying a message that God, too, hears and understands.

Assurance that God has heard and cares

The sufferer hopes that God still cares, that God has not turned his back on the one who most needs him. If one has prayed to God for the suffering to go away but the situation remains unchanged, how is one to know that God has listened and cares? Even if our prayers are not answered in some spectacular return to health and happiness, we at least want to know that God is still with us and knows how things are going for us. If only we knew that, we could manage to cope with the suffering which we must continue to bear.

Job wanted to have an encounter with God. He wanted God to tell him why he was suffering, to point out to him what had caused it so that he could make a change and allow the suffering to go away. Finally, after what must have seemed a terribly long time, God spoke out of the whirlwind and confronted Job. But God did not directly answer Job's questions; they were side-stepped. Instead, God said, "A human being can never know the answer to such mysteries as why humans suffer. It is impertinent to think that you should find answers. You must trust me to take care of those things that are beyond your powers of comprehension."

Job had thought that he wanted intellectual answers that would finally make sense out of his suffering. That was his hope for what would come out of an encounter with God. Instead, what Job received was the assurance that God loved him and had been listening to him and feeling with him all along. Now Job was certain that God cared, and this was enough to sustain him. Now he could even bear his suffering, because he knew that God would be with him. Later on, Job had his fortunes restored, but in the meantime as he waited for the suffering to go away, it was surely more bearable, because he was able to hope in a God who hears and who cares.

In the person of Jesus we have an even better model of a God who is present in our suffering and hears us as we cry from our pain. In Jesus we have a God who is willing to bear suffering with us and for us. Jesus could not avoid the cross, just as we cannot avoid all the sufferings of life. As Jesus found hope in the presence of a God who was with him in that ordeal, we can find hope in the caring and suffering God who accompanies us in our moments of suffering that, for one reason or other, cannot be avoided.

God will defeat evil and suffering once and for all

Suffering is not forever. No matter how hopeless things appear to us now, God will have the last word. God is good and will see that eventually everything will be all right. Though the events of Good Friday may almost drown us in gloom, we know that there is an Easter. We have the sign of victory. Though the present torment is real, we have caught the glimpse of the final defeat of all things that mean to harm us, and we take hope in that.

God's will is for the good of all God's creatures, and God's will is not going to be thwarted. All through the Bible we read how God has rescued his people out of hopeless situations. Sometimes God has even taken the awful things that happen to us and turned them into something good. In the midst of suffering, it may sometimes seem as if there were no end, no way out, and we cry, "How long, O Lord?" At those times, it is a powerful word of hope to know that God will win the final victory. Suffering is not the normal state of affairs, and God will not leave us forever in that state.

The promise of life beyond this one

We have an important final hope to fall back on. The suffering of the present life may torment us continually. We may even suffer until the time of our death. During the course of our suffering we will be comforted by the support of other human beings and by the presence of a God who cares. But our belief in a God who will win the final victory over all suffering would be hollow indeed if this life is all there is. If you can promise me no relief from suffering until the time of my death, that is scant hope unless there is the possibility of further existence following my death. Sufferers need the hope of an eternal life, because sometimes the suffering of the present life will not go away and the only possibility of a better life will have to come in a new creation after this one has run its course.

And so we are sustained in our present suffering by our belief in life after death. We dream of a time of peace, of health, of closeness to God, when anxiety and pain and fear and suffering are all relegated to the distant past. Even when forces of evil and corruption seem to have the upper hand, we can still live in hope, because we know that this world is not all there is and that God will gain the final victory. Since Jesus rose from the dead, we know that we, too, will be born into a new life. God will forgive our sin and take away our pain, and there will be joy forever.

In the meantime, suffering remains. We cannot excuse or belittle the pain and suffering of the present world by holding up the promise of a better world to come. We are called on to help eliminate the causes of suffering and to minister to those whose suffering goes on relentlessly. We can answer their hopes for a compassionate friend. We can help point them to a God who hears and cares.

And, above all, we can proclaim the promise of a God who, through Jesus Christ our Lord, has gained the victory over everything that can hurt us—even the greatest enemy, death itself.

Now that is something in which to put our hope.